Phetheni Lorrai

FISH
NEXT DOOR

Copyright © 2024 Phetheni Lorraine Ndhlovu.

All rights reserved. No part of this book may be used or reproduced by any means, graphic, electronic, or mechanical, including photocopying, recording, taping or by any information storage retrieval system without the written permission of the author except in the case of brief quotations embodied in critical articles and reviews.

LifeRich Publishing is a registered trademark of The Reader's Digest Association, Inc.

LifeRich Publishing books may be ordered through booksellers or by contacting:

LifeRich Publishing
1663 Liberty Drive
Bloomington, IN 47403
www.liferichpublishing.com
844-686-9607

Because of the dynamic nature of the Internet, any web addresses or links contained in this book may have changed since publication and may no longer be valid. The views expressed in this work are solely those of the author and do not necessarily reflect the views of the publisher, and the publisher hereby disclaims any responsibility for them.

Any people depicted in stock imagery provided by Getty Images are models, and such images are being used for illustrative purposes only.
Certain stock imagery © Getty Images.

Illustrated by Barbara C. Syring © 2024
Design by RAK Design © 2024

ISBN: 978-1-4897-5093-8 (sc)
ISBN: 978-1-4897-5092-1 (e)

Print information available on the last page.

LifeRich Publishing rev. date: 07/24/2024

This book is dedicated to Somopho Primary School of Macekane, KwaZulu Natal, South Africa.

Table Contents

Fish found in the Puget Sound & Pacific Northwest 1

Talk to Text 2

Types of Fish/Food/Habitat/Predators

Salmon 4

Ratfish 9

Dogfish 11

Spiny Lumpsucker 15

Rockfish 17

Pacific Cod 18

Skate Fish 18

Special Friends and Fish Stories 21

Terminologies 26

References 27

Acknowledgments 28

About the Author 31

Hi friends!

My name is Salmon. I am going to tell you a little bit about the type of fish found in the Pacific Northwest.

The Pacific Northwest is located here:

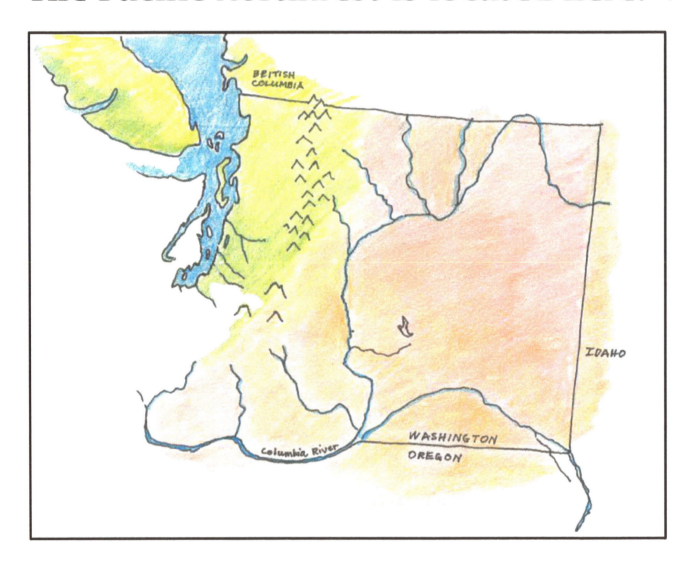

Get a pencil, as we are going to be talking to each other, and I will be asking you some questions. We are going to apply a reading skill, called "talk to a text." This is where a reader does just that! The reader talks to a text, highlights a book, makes some comments, and asks questions.

This skill makes reading a book fun. Look at the example below:

> Interesting! I didn't know that.
>
> Get a pencil, as we are going to be talking to each other, and I will be asking you some questions. We are going to apply a reading skill, called talk to a text. This is where a reader does just that! The reader talks to a text, highlights a book, makes some comments, and asks questions. This skill makes reading a book fun.
>
> **Are you ready?** Hh... mm talk to a text? I wonder what does that mean? How do I talk to book? It does not talk back to me!
> Yes, I am 🙂
>
> Before we start, I would like us to [recognize] acknowledge God, who created the ocean, and all the fish found in the world. Genesis is the first book in the Bible
> Genesis 1:21 reads, "So God created the large sea animals. He created all the many living things in the sea, and every kind of bird that flies in the air. And God saw that this was good." (ERV)
>
> How did God create all fish and ocean? Oh I see, God created all fish and the ocean based on his word (the Bible).
>
> Cool that God created many living things.
>
> Yes! God created me too.
>
> talk to a text sounds to me like I'm thinking out loud, except I'm writing my thoughts down. Why do I have to do that? Is it so that I could remember what I was thinking when I was reading? Cool! Let's do this!

Are you ready?

Before we start, I would like us to acknowledge God, who created the ocean, and all the fish found in the world.

Genesis 1:21 reads, *"So God created the large sea animals. He created all the many living things in the sea and every kind of bird that flies in the air. And God saw that this was good"* (ERV).

**Thank you, Lord
for your creation!**

I would like you to thank God for all His creation too. You are welcome to thank Him for any personal gift as well.

What are you thankful for?

_____

_____

_____

My name is Salmon.

What is your name?
_____

Can you tell me little bit about yourself, anything that comes to mind?
_____
_____
_____

Where do you live?
_____
_____
_____

Salmon: Habitat

I (Salmon) live in many places. For example, I may be found in lakes and rivers, which are full of fresh water. As a baby, I live in fresh water. As I grow older, I migrate to the ocean, which is salt water. I can even be found in Everett, Washington, which is in the Puget Sound area. I am also in many parts of the Salish Sea.

Here is an example of the life cycle of a salmon.

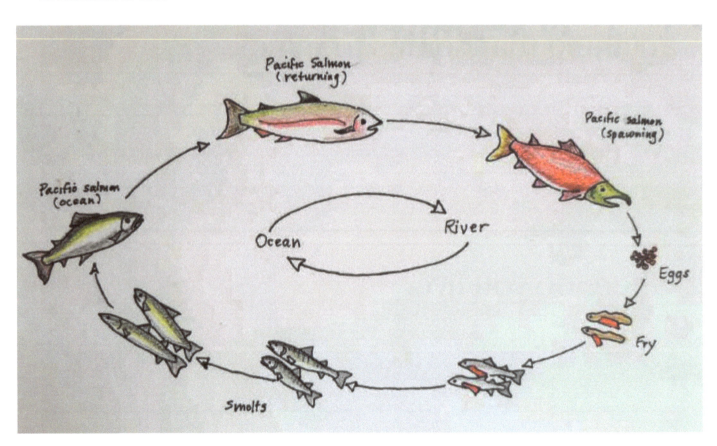

Draw one here:

Salmon: Predator

Do you know who my enemies are? I am afraid of you! Do you want to know why? Often, I am found on your dinner table. Have you ever eaten salmon before? You see? That is why I am afraid of you!

I am also afraid of BIG fish, like sharks. I am really afraid of sharks because they are big. They are like the kings of the oceans.

Salmon: Food

Guess what I eat?

I eat small fish like Capelin.
What do you eat?

This is what Capelin looks like. I drew a fish.

Can you draw me too?

Now, I would like to introduce you to my new friend, the Ratfish. Say, what? Rat and fish at the same time? Yep! That's his name alright.

Hi, my name is Ratfish!

My friend Salmon told me all about himself. He told me where he lives, who he is afraid of, and what he likes to eat.

Ratfish: Habitat

Can you guess where I live?

I live in the mud in the beautiful Pacific Ocean. Yes, I know that's funny, but that is where my home is.

Ratfish: Predator

I am afraid of Dogfish, Sharks, and other big fish.

Ratfish: Food

I like to eat crabs, and some other hard-shelled sea creatures. Have you eaten crabs before? I like to eat seafood found at the bottom of the ocean because I live in the mud.

Now, I would like to introduce you to my new friend, the Dogfish.

Hi friends, my name is Dogfish!

My friend Ratfish told me a lot about all of you. What did you like about my friend?

Oh really? He told you that?

Dogfish: Habitat
I live in the North Pacific Ocean and North Atlantic Ocean. I might be in your neighborhood.

Do you live near an ocean? _____

Dogfish: Predator

RUN FOR YOUR LIFE!

I must worry about being eaten by larger sharks, seals, and orca whales. So, I swim for my life because those guys are humungous!

FEAR NOT!

I know I must swim for my life from the big creatures in the ocean, but I must not be afraid! Beware of your environment, and the good Lord will protect you from danger.

The Bible reads, *"Don't be afraid, for I am with you. Don't be discouraged, for I am your God. I will strengthen you and help you. I will hold you up with my victorious right hand"* (Isaiah 41:10, NLT).

God has got your back!

Is there anything that you would like God to protect you from? This is where you may talk or pray to Him about anything.

Dogfish: Food

Guess what's for dinner tonight? I might eat shrimp, crab, and other fish that are smaller than me. What are you having for dinner tonight? **Draw it below.**

It was very nice to meet you. Now I would like to introduce you to my new friend, Spiny Lumpsucker.

Spiny Lumpsucker: Habitat

Hello friends! My name is Spiny Lumpsucker. I know you are probably thinking I like to suck lollipops: no, I do not! I was named Lumpsucker because I am lumpy like Play-Doh. I can be found in the cold waters of the Arctic, North Atlantic, and North Pacific oceans. You can also meet me anytime, right here in Puget Sound!

Spiny Lumpsucker Predators:

I am always watching out for Pacific Cod, Sablefish, and Lancetfish.

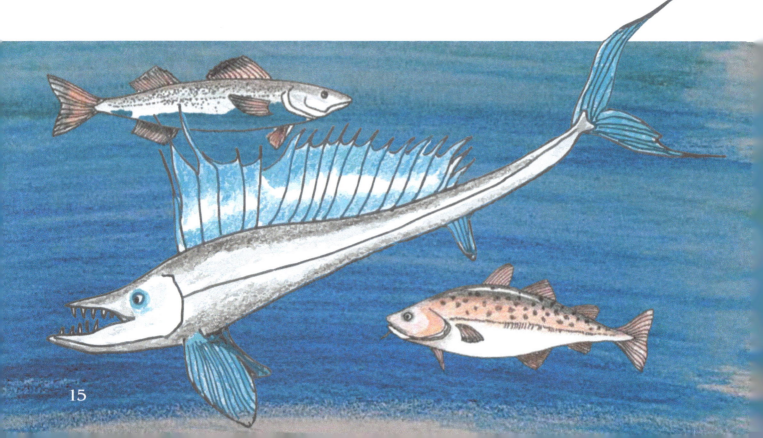

Spiny Lumpsucker: Food

I like to eat slow moving crustaceans, worms, and mollusks.

"Lobster"

Fun fact: *Guess what?*
Do you want to hear a fun fact about me? Research done by the University of Washington mentioned that "the Lumpsucker is a poor swimmer..." (2002).

Do you know how to swim? Well, if not, don't feel bad. You are not alone. There are some adults that don't know how to swim either. But, if you don't know how to swim, I encourage you to learn. It's a useful skill to have in life.

And now, I would like to introduce you to another fishy relative who lives in the cooler waters of the Northwest.

Ahoy! I am called Rockfish!

I have a quiz for you. As my name suggests, do I live under a rock, or do I rock all night under the sea? If you pick yes for any of the above, you are ... funny, but wrong.

I can live to be 20 years old. This means I am a granny in the fish family.

I am well respected and in return, I tell lots of stories and give wise advice.

Do you know the life expectancy of a fish?

Here comes the Pacific Cod!

Hail, little friends! It's nice to surface back once more for some sunlight. Boy! It's so sunny! I may go blind. You know, I live  deeeeeeeep down in the ocean where no one can see me.

Salmon says, "Some people think that cod is very tasty; especially when served with chips. You should give it a try, and let me know what you think."

I would like to introduce you to my new friend who goes by the name of Skate Fish. Skate Fish isn't a steak, don't make that mistake.

Skate Fish: Food

Skates also eat other fish, as well as octopus, crab, and lobster (Longe, Nemeh, Nicholson, and Skates, 2021). Doesn't that sound like a delicious dinner?

Have you eaten octopus, crab, or lobster before?

_____

After what you just read, which one was your favorite fish, and why?

_____

_____

_____

Draw your special fish.

That's all friends!

I am glad to show you all my friends, and the ocean. {Yawn} Thank you for going on this deep-sea adventure with me. It was surely nautical.

{Yawn}

It's time for bed.

Sweet dreams.

Zzzzzzz.......

The Author's Special Friends and Fish Stories

Readers, now I want to introduce you to a family friend, and my son's mentor. This is Mr. Dan Templeman, the retired Chief of Police in Everett, Washington. I asked him what his favorite fish was, and he told me that he absolutely LOVES Northwest Salmon.

In the Templeman Family, one of the sons is a chef. The Chief mentioned that his son is a really great chef.

 Dr. Paul E. Pitre says the whale is his favorite! "I like the whale, because they are gentle giants.

Here in the Pacific Northwest, you can see them swimming in Puget Sound.

They have spouts they use to breathe when they come to the surface. They also blow out water through their spouts, and it's like a cascade of water. If you get too close, you could get a shower!

The whale has been an important fish for our indigenous tribes, or our Native American Sisters and Brothers. They have a special connection to the land and sea.

Whales are mammals and very smart. A whale can be as long as 100 feet.

Scientists have studied the whale extensively. They want to know how whales communicate. Whales have been studied for many years."

Please meet my other friends. This is the Fernandes Family. Their favorite fish is salmon. Every time I visit, they prepare my favorite fish. Pradeep has shared how to prepare the dish on the next page, and would like you to try it.

Thank you, Pradeep.

Pictured: From the left is Janet, Pradeep, and Kina.

My family and friends who LOVE salmon!

Pictured left: Back row, My son Sibusiso Ndhlovu, Asanda and Siyabonga with Mbi up front.

Pradeep's Salmon Recipe

- 1 lb. King Salmon
- Half a lemon, squeeze and rub
- 1/2 Teaspoon salt to taste
- Marinate for 15 minutes
- 1/2 Tablespoon Fresh Dill Weed, sprinkle on Salmon
- Slice half a lemon, and lay three to four slices on Salmon
- Heat oven to 400°F
- Bake Salmon for 20-25 minutes until the salmon slides off the skin
- When baked, sprinkle more fresh Dill Weed on the Salmon
- Cut about six more slices of lemon, remove the ones that were used to bake and replace with fresh lemon slices

Enjoy!

Everyone! My name is Lucy Little. That is my true last name, not because I am little. How coincidental is that?

I will tell you about my favorite foods. I like to beg for left over pizza from my parents. I also eat my ordinary dog chow. Hmmm! Yum! I do not eat grapes, chocolate cake, or candies because it will hurt my body.

In fact, NEVER feed dogs the foods listed, because it will damage their liver, kidneys, heart, and other major organs.

Ask a veterinarian for more information.

These are my friend's stories. Now, ask your friend what their favorite fish is.

So, there you have it. Salmon it is! Salmon for the money! Salmon for the protein! *KING SALMON* all the way!

You can now guess the popularity of Salmon. I like Salmon, you like Salmon, she likes Salmon, and so does most of my family, friends and colleagues. For those of you that don' t like Salmon, perhaps you need to reconsider.

Salmon is always King.

Terminologies

Crustaceans: Any of a large class of mostly water-dwelling arthropods, (such as lobsters, shrimp, crabs, wood lice, water fleas, and barnacles), having an exoskeleton of chitin, and a compound of calcium

Estuaries: a semi-enclosed coastal body of water that has a free connection with the open sea and within which seawater is measurably diluted with fresh water

Habitat: the home of an animal or a plant

Humongous: extremely large

Mollusks: Any of a large phylum of invertebrate animals, (such as snails, clams, and octopus), with a soft body, lacking segments, and usually enclosed in a shell containing calcium

Predator: an animal that obtains food mostly by killing and eating other animals

Salish Sea: a large estuary on the Pacific Northwest Coast that represents a great tidal stream resource because of its strong tidal currents in many tidal channels

Salt Water: water to which salt, (such as sodium chloride), has been added

References

Bible Hub. Isaiah 41:10 Retrieved from: https://biblehub.com/isaiah/41-10.htm.

Brach. R, Deb. M, Xiao. Z, Wang. T, & Yang. Z. (2021). Tidal Stream Energy Resource Characterization in the Salish Sea. Renewable Energy, 172, 188-20. Retrieved from: https://doi.org/10.1016/j.- renene.2021.03.028

Britannica Kids Dictionary, Encyclopedia Britannica, Inc., 2022, Retrieved from: https://kids.britannica.com/kids/browse/dictionary.

Britannica Kids. (n.d.). https://kids.britannica.com/kids/search/dictionary?query=crustaceans

Genesis 1:21 (ERV). (n.d.). Bible Gateway. https://www.biblegateway.com/passage/?search= Genesis+1%3A21&version=ERV

Merriam-Webster. (n.d.). Humongous definition & meaning. Merriam-Webster. Retrieved from https://www.merriam-webster.com/- dictionary/humongous?src=search-dict- box

Longe (Eds.), Nemeh & J. L., Nicholson, F. C., Skates. In K. H., (2021) The Gale Encyclopedia of Science (6th ed., Vol. 7, pp. 4031-4032). Gale. Retrieved from: https://link.gale.com/apps/doc/CX8124402240/SCIC?u=sirlsmain&sid=bookmarkSCIC&xid=8c56949c

Report Summarizes Morphology Study Findings from University of Washington (Pacific Spiny Lumpsucker Armor-development, Damage, and Defense in the Intertidal). (2022). Science Letter, 906. https://link.gale.com/apps/doc/A690967173/CSIC? u=sirls_-main&sid=bookmarkCSIC&x

Acknowledgments

I would like to thank my Marine Biology Pacific Northwest Professor, Shannon Call from the Everett Community College. One day she told me I would do great things. I remember being so frustrated and all I could do was cry. Thank you for your gifted ears, and your time. I did not want a solution, just someone that would listen, and you did.

Many thanks to Teresa Jones, Associate Faculty Librarian at Everett Community College. Thank you, Ms. Teresa, and the Staff, for being so approachable. I enjoyed doing my research while attending Everett Community College.

Dr. Tolulola Bayode, how do I thank you?

Thank you so much for your friendship, wealth of knowledge, and contribution to my first book. I appreciate your love for Africa, the underserved community.

Barbara Syring, my sister in Christ; I have seen God through your love and action. Thank you for representing the Christian Community so well.

May our Lord Jesus smile at you and your family.

Professor Kathy Johnson, thank you! Your teaching of "talk to a text" has inspired me. My hope is readers use this technique to bring text alive.

Special thanks to Ms. Bette Bell from Edmonds, WA, my friend who taught English as a foreign language.

Thank you, Ndhlovu Family for your prayers. Anongibeka! (It's a family joke), that means "pray for me."

Rebecca Kizziar, I am out of words. You are a Godsend. I owe you the highest honor ceremony in South Africa. Mark my word: it will happen by the grace of God.

College Sandy and all the volunteers at the Everett Community College BRIDGES Center, thank you for volunteering your precious time by giving back to the community your wealth of knowledge. May our good Lord bless you all with a long life.

About the Author

The author's name is Phetheni Ndhlovu. She is a born-again Christian who loves God with all her heart, mind, and soul. She is also the proud mother of her son, Sibusiso. As a philanthropist, she absolutely loves to help underprivileged students.

Born and raised in South Africa, in a small village called Macekane. Phetheni is grateful for her mother's prayers, and her father's words of wisdom. One piece of advice she learned from her father was "Anobhekana MaNdhlovu" meaning: "you must watch out for one another, Ndhlovu."

One day Phetheni had a dream about her father. He told her to go back to school, as she had dropped out of college in the past. She is proud to announce that she graduated with an Associate in Arts Degree from Everett Community College in Summer, 2022. In her further studies, Phetheni earned her Bachelor of Arts Degree in Human Services from Western Washington University in Spring, 2024.

To God alone be the glory for the things He has done, and will continue to do!